QUINOA AND GLUTEN-FREE COOKBOOK MADE SIMPLE

+ 40 HEALTHY & GREAT-TASTING RECIPES. | EAT GREAT, LOSE WEIGHT AND FEEL HEALTHY.

PAMELA KENDRICK

CONTENTS

Introduction   vii

1. What Is Quinoa?   1

POPULAR VEGAN RECIPES THAT USE QUINOA

1. Quinoa and Black Beans   15
2. Lemon and Spinach Quinoa Bake   17
3. Quinoa-Gnocchi Potato Salad   20
4. Quinoa Salad with Black and White Beans   23
5. Tropical Breakfast Quinoa   28

POPULAR CHICKEN RECIPES THAT USE QUINOA

6. Yummy Chicken Burritos   33
7. Quinoa Stir Fry   35
8. Greek Pita   38
9. Mexican Fiesta   40
10. Quesadilla   42
11. Quinoa and Beans   44

POPULAR BEEF RECIPES THAT USE QUINOA

12. Grilled Beef Tenderloin with Leek Tomato Quinoa and Roasted Garlic Sauce   49
13. Leek-Tomato Quinoa   51
14. Beef Stir Fry with Quinoa   53

POPULAR SEAFOOD RECIPES THAT USE QUINOA

15. Salad Quinoa Seafood	57
16. Salmon Quinoa Cakes	60
17. Quinoa with Roasted Fish and Veggies	63

POPULAR PORK (OR LAMB) RECIPES THAT USE QUINOA

18. Pork (or lamb) Fried Quinoa	69
19. Pork Tenderloin with Quinoa Pilaf	71
20. Pork Quinoa Soup	73
21. Quinoa and Ham Omelets	76

2. Gluten Free	78

MAIN DISH GLUTEN FREE RECIPES.

22. Lamb with Yams and Apples	89
23. Cheesy Mexican Chicken	92
24. Broiled Steak Salad	94
25. Hearty Steak and Cheese Soup	96
26. Beef and Broccoli	99
27. Curried Chicken and Mango Summer Salad	102

SIDE DISHES AND VEGETABLES

28. Winter Squash in Brown Butter and Parsley	107
29. Chinese Green Beans	109
30. High Energy Breakfast Smoothie	111
31. Heart Healthy Spinach Side Salad	113
32. Creamy Broccoli and Cauliflower Salad	116
33. Hearty Summer Salad	118

APPETIZERS AND SNACKS

34. Garlic and Parmesan Chicken Wings	123
35. Hot and Spicy Chicken Wings	125
36. Gluten Free Conserves and Relishes	128
37. Raw Salsa	129
38. Home Made Spicy Salsa	130
39. Cranberry Conserve	132

GLUTEN FREE DESSERTS

40. Hot Chocolate Pudding	137
41. Rice Pudding	139
42. Chocolate Fondue	141
43. Chocolate Cake	143
44. Baked Apples	146
45. Coffee Chocolate Mousse	149
Gluten Free Tips for Fun Kid Foods	151
Crock Pot Cookery and Gluten Free?	155
Tips on Living Gluten Free	159
References	161

© **Copyright 2021 by Pamela Kendrick - All rights reserved.**

This document is geared towards providing exact and reliable information in regards to the topic and issue covered. The publication is sold with the idea that the publisher is not required to render accounting, officially permitted, or otherwise, qualified services. If advice is necessary, legal or professional, a practiced individual in the profession should be ordered.

- From a Declaration of Principles which was accepted and approved equally by a Committee of the American Bar Association and a Committee of Publishers and Associations.

In no way is it legal to reproduce, duplicate, or transmit any part of this document in either electronic means or in printed format. Recording of this publication is strictly prohibited and any storage of this document is not allowed unless with written permission from the publisher. All rights reserved.

The information provided herein is stated to be truthful and consistent, in that any liability, in terms of inattention or otherwise, by any usage or abuse of any policies, processes, or directions contained within is the solitary and utter responsibility of the recipient reader. Under no circumstances will any legal responsibility or blame be held against the publisher for any reparation, damages, or monetary loss due to the information herein, either directly or indirectly.

Respective authors own all copyrights not held by the publisher.

The information herein is offered for informational purposes solely, and is universal as so. The presentation of the information is without contract or any type of guarantee assurance.

The trademarks that are used are without any consent, and the publication of the trademark is without permission or backing by the trademark owner.

All trademarks and brands within this book are for clarifying purposes only and are the owned by the owners themselves, not affiliated with this document.

INTRODUCTION

In this book you will find two sections of very healthy and beneficial diets in the Quinoa diet and the Gluten Free diet. Each diet uses recipes that replace the need for wheat gluten. The Quinoa uses quinoa and discusses the benefits and history of this plant. The Gluten Free diet uses other ingredients to replace wheat flour such as arrowroot, tapioca and even nut flours. The

Introduction

purpose of this book is to show a healthy alternative to the fad diets out today and offer better choices.

Quinoa comes from a plant in the goosefoot family. The goosefoot family keeps great company with vegetables such as beets and spinach. Quinoa is not a "grassy" plant, nor is it a legume (bean or pea). It is very much similar to buckwheat. The seeds go a long way in producing enough food to feed many. One pound of seeds yields an entire acre of quinoa. This can feed 3,650 people, just from one pound of seeds, so it is a very economical food.

Quinoa has been around feeding people for well over 3,000 years dating back to the ancient Inca people of South America. The grain like plant can thrive in the worst of conditions even to growing in the high cool altitudes of the Andes Mountains. Quinoa made resurgence in the 1970's with the suggestion of the spiritual Bolivian teacher to his students and the focus on meditation. The UN saw the benefit in quinoa and they declare it a super food.

The health benefits of quinoa exceed that of most grains. Quinoa contains some very healthy phytonutrients that are show the ability to reduce inflammation in the body.

The promise of benefits extends to that of lab animals where quinoa helped to treat obesity successfully, especially helpful in maintaining weight loss too.

Quinoa was used by ancient civilizations for its medicinal qualities as well as for a beneficial filling food.

Today the health benefits known for eating quinoa are wide. First, it helps with digestive system issues. Second, it helps to reduce high blood pressure. These two benefits alone make this the perfect food for many who suffer from these health conditions. Quinoa is a perfect food to go with the gluten free diet. Vegans and vegetarians also love to include quinoa in their diets. The biggest difference in quinoa from grains is the high levels of amino acids, making it a much healthier choice for recipes that call for grains.

Quinoa has benefits that go beyond filling the belly and

Introduction

making one feel satisfied after a meal. The medicinal benefits are icing on the cake, so to speak. It does not harm people; it will not be like an overdose of medication if eaten, it is a perfectly safe food to include in a diet plan, safe for children and adults alike.

Vegans love to use quinoa in their diets because of the high amino acid content. It makes for a great meat or protein substitute. Vegans and vegetarians can enjoy the Quinoa Chili. Also included in this book for vegans are recipes for Quinoa and Black Beans, Lemon and Spinach Quinoa Bake, Quinoa Gnocchi Potato Salad, Quinoa Salad with Black and White Beans and the tasty Tropical Breakfast Quinoa.

For chicken lovers there are five recipes included with chicken as the main ingredient. Try the Yummy Chicken Burritos or the Quinoa Stir Fry. Chicken is one of the healthiest of meats and pairing it with quinoa makes it a winner for a main entree. Also, try the Greek Pita, Mexican Fiesta and the Quinoa and Beans.

Even beef goes well with quinoa. Try the Grilled Beef Tenderloin with Leek Tomato Quinoa and Roasted Garlic Sauce or the Leek Tomato Quinoa. If you cook with lean cuts of meat, even beef, you will cut out a lot of the bad fats often associated with beef food choices. Try the Beef Stir Fry with Quinoa for a delicious healthy meal.

For seafood lovers there are four recipes using quinoa with seafood including shrimp and salmon. Fish is high in omega threes that are very beneficial to the brain and the immune system. Try the Mediterranean Seafood Salad with Quinoa, Salmon Quinoa Cakes, Quinoa with Roasted Fish and Veggies and the Shrimp and Quinoa Croquettes with Sauce.

Even pork goes well with quinoa. The right cuts of pork can be low in fat, just watch the fat content, and purchase accordingly. Quinoa is so healthy and tasty it can go well with even pork. Try the Pork Fried Quinoa. This recipe can be tailored to use lamb too. Try the Pork Tenderloin with Quinoa Pilaf, Pork Quinoa Soup and the Quinoa and Ham Omelets (great for breakfast or supper!)

Introduction

The Gluten Free section is for people who are going gluten free either by choice or by necessity. The gluten free diet helps people to overcome gluten intolerances and allergies as well as offers a great way to lose weight and maintain weight loss. Some choose the diet simply because it is very healthy and beneficial. Choose from many great gluten free recipes.

This recipe book enables a person on a gluten free diet to plan meals for weeks, including desserts. The main and side dishes offer a wide variety and flavors. Choose from Garlic and Parmesan Chicken Wings or Hot and Spicy Chicken Wings. There are Raw Salsa and Home Made Spicy Salsa. Try the Hearty Summer Salad, Creamy Broccoli and Cauliflower Salad or the Heart Healthy Spinach Side Salad.

Now for the gluten free desserts and snacks, do not worry, the taste and flavor are not skimped. Try the Hot Chocolate Pudding, Dark Chocolate Fondue, Coffee Chocolate Mousse, Gluten Free Chocolate Chip Cookies and the Fast and Easy Gluten Free Rice Pudding. There are even suggestions for more gluten free snacks and treats especially for children. Further included are tips on gluten free living, how to eat at restaurants and remain gluten free.

1

WHAT IS QUINOA?

About the Grain

Its scientific name is Chenopodium quinoa, and it has recently gained popularity as a grain of high nutritional value.

Quinoa is an annual plant which is a type of weed related to the goosefoot family. It is also closely related to the family of plants that includes spinach, table beet, and sugar beets and is susceptible to the same issues as these crops while growing. Unlike grassy grain plants, the quinoa has broadleaf and is not a legume but has a similar structure to buckwheat.

It is a remarkably efficient plant to harvest and just one pound of seeds is enough to harvest a whole acre of the crop. This was able to sustain an Andean family of ten for a whole year.

Quinoa History

The origins of Quinoa date back over 3,000 to the ancient Incan civilizations of South America. The indigenous tribes in the

Andes area of Peru, Colombia, Chile, and Bolivia used it as a staple grain in their diet.

It is one of the few grains that is able to survive the high altitudes of the region and the harshness of the Andes climate. This area is subject to intense sun,
   drought, and occasional frost as well. All of these conditions the hearty grain was able to withstand for thousands of years. Its strength was admired by the Ancient Incans who called it "mother grain" and treated its harvest with religious reverence.

During the 16th century Spanish invaders came to the Andes region and forbid the growing of quinoa which was seen as "Indian food". They favored the assimilation of the "savage" natives into their culture and so corn and potatoes took quinoa's place. However, the grain endured and grew in the wild so that we could enjoy it today.

The modern popularity of quinoa can be traced back to the 1970's when Oscar Ichazo, a Bolivian spiritual teacher, encouraged students to eat the grain as an aid to meditation. This began its rise in popularity in the Western World where even the United Nations has declared it a "super food."

Health Benefits

Studies in recent history have shown that the phytonutrients in quinoa has anti inflammatory properties. The combination of properties has been shown to reduce conditions such as obesity in lab animals when fed on a regular basis as a preventative measure. These anti inflammatory phytonutrients include; Arabians, hydroxybenzoic acids, hydroxycinnamic, flavanoids, saponins, omega-3 fatty acid, and alpha-linolenic acid (ALA) it is higher in healthy fats than other cereal grains and is shown to help reduce cholesterol.

Nutritionally, a ⅓ cup of cooked quinoa contains 160 calories, 2.5 grams of fat and 6 grams of protein.

Quinoa also contains antioxidant phytonutrients in a high enough amount to be compared to those in cranberry and lingonberry. Unlike other grains, quinoa is a great source of protein, comparable even to that of milk. It also contains twice the amount of calcium found in whole wheat. Other vitamins that quinoa contains are; iron, phosphorous, and B vitamins. Also found in high amounts in quinoa members of the vitamin E family, especially gamma-tocopherol. Another benefit of quinoa is its tolerance for those with other grain allergies. For those with gluten intolerances, quinoa is commonly suggested as a replacement for the traditional wheat. It is easily digestible which makes it highly desirable for the sensitive digestive tracts of those with allergies and also children.

Besides the nutritional value of quinoa, Incans used it as medicine as well. Ground quinoa was cooked down and used to treat a variety of ailments such as; appendicitis, tuberculosis, and motion sickness. It was also used as a diuretic and to induce vomiting. Its strength was believed to help build bones and strengthen mothers before and after birth, long before its high calcium content was discovered by scientists.

The super food benefits of quinoa are easy to incorporate into a healthy diet. The grain can be purchased in bulk and stored in bins. When shopping for quinoa in bulk ensure the source containers are free of moisture.

Quinoa is a grain that expands greatly when prepared and so this should be taken into consideration when deciding on how much to purchase at a time. It can be stored in a dry container for 6 months in the refrigerator without losing nutritional value. The most common variety of quinoa is an off-white color however you may also see the black or red colored types. Stores may also combine the three in one bulk bin allowing you to enjoy the variety of all.

Quinoa's popularity among the gluten free enthusiasts has led to it being available in flour form as well. It is highly digestible and can be used as a complete substitute for flour in recipes. However, usually it is combined with other gluten free flour such as tapioca or rice.

The internet is full of recipes using quinoa. The general way to cook the grain is to boil it with water in a ration of 2:1. Once it reaches a boil the heat should be reduced and allowed to simmer while covered. Cooking it with this boiling method takes only 15 minutes. To enhance the nutty flavor of quinoa the grain can be dry roasted before cooking. For dry roasting it is heated in a skillet over medium-high heat for a couple of minutes before boiling.

What Are The Health Benefits Found In Quinoa

There are several health benefits to Quinoa, pronounced keen-wah or Ken-noh-a, when this grain like seed is incorporated into a regular meal plan or recipe. The possible health benefits range from relief from stomach and digestive system discomfort to a reduction in blood pressure.

First and foremost Quinoa is perfect for those on a gluten free diet. Quinoa is a not a grain. It is a seed from plants that are in the same family as beets, spinach and even tumbleweeds. Because it is a seed and not a grain it is naturally gluten free. Those on a gluten free diet can incorporate Quinoa in their diets as a type of faux grain. This is possible because of many of the grain like characteristics that quinoa has. Quinoa can be used as an ingredient similar to flour in recipes order to make breads, pastries, cookies and more.

The ability to substitute Quinoa as a grain in specialized recipes allow people with a gluten intolerance the ability to avoid stomach and digestive problems that are often associated with their condition. Gluten free diets are also often associated with those who are lactose intolerant or following a lactose free diet.

Quinoa is a wonderful addition to menu planning for people following a vegetarian, vegan or any other type of low or non-meat diet. This is because Quinoa is a source for natural protein that is plant based instead of animal based. Grains are not considered to be a proper protein source. This is because grains have low amino acids levels pertaining to lysine and isoleucine. Since Quinoa is a seed and not a grain it has higher levels of lysine and isoleucine which is what
is needed for a protein source to be considered a "complete" protein source.

A single 3.5 ounce serving of prepared Quinoa contains upwards of 14 grams of protein. This may help solve any issues that some dieters may have of not getting enough protein when following any style of vegetarian diet. The ability to take in protein can help reduce the possible need for processed over the counter protein supplements. The quality of such protein supplements can vary greatly between manufactures.

. . .

It should be noted that many types of beans and lentils are higher in protein, per prepared serving, than Quinoa. However; the ability to use Quinoa in a large variety of dishes and as a faux grain, as well as with the additional benefits listed in this article, have helped increase its popularity.

Along with high levels of protein Quinoa is also rich in fiber which is often recommended in healthy diets. A single 3.5 ounce serving of prepared Quinoa contains 7 grams of dietary fiber. This combination of protein and dietary fiber is yet another benefit for those people fighting issues related to dietary tract problems that are associated with gluten intolerances and or being lactose intolerant.

Quinoa also contains nine essential amino acids. The nine essential amino acids are histidine, lysine, leucine, methionine, isloleucine, tryptophan, threonine, valine and phenylalanine. The nine essential amino acids are required by the human body but can only be obtained through digesting food or through supplements. This is because the human body does not synthesize them as it does with other amino acids. This combination of protein, fiber and amino acids makes Quinoa a perfect substitution for animal protein and is a factor in making it easy to digest.

Quinoa is also rich in complex carbohydrates which digest gradually. This gives the body time to absorb nutrients slows the conversion to sugar and fat. Complex carbohydrates also keep you feeling full longer which may keep some from overeating.

Quinoa also contains heart healthy fats. Almost one fourth of is fatty acid is in the form of oleic acid which is a heart-healthy monounsaturated fat. In addition another 8% of quinoa's fatty acid is in the form of omega-3 fatty acids known as alpha-linolenic acid or ALA.

Quinoa also includes elements associated with vitamin E that have been linked to anti-inflammatory relief in health research. Quinoa is also a natural source of nutrients such as folate, copper as well as the mineral Calcium all of which are lacking in whole wheat. Magnesium and iron are also found in quinoa which may lower blood pressure in some people.

While seemingly exploding onto the health food and whole food arena quinoa has a long history. Quinoa can be traced to the Peruvian Andes where it was produced for consumption by the Incas over 5,000 years ago. Upon the arrival of the Spanish the widespread cultivation of quinoa rapidly declined. The Spanish invaders may have considered quinoa as being lowly and wheat was introduced to the local population.

Quinoa has a slight to heavy bitter or soapy taste associated with the natural presence of saponin which is a protective coating. The taste is reduced in most forms of commercial quinoa and with the cooking process. One fear associated with processed quinoa is that the nutritional benefits of the seed may be reduced the more processed the final product is. This has not proven to be the case but many people prefer to remove the possibility of a bitter taste with rinsing and light toasting.

Quinoa can be introduced into diet in a variety of ways ranging from a lightly toasted snack food similar to sunflower seeds to an ingredient for use in baking healthier items including bread, cookies, brownies and more.

How Does Quinoa Help One to Eat Healthy?

As people look to eat healthier foods, quinoa is really making its presence known in the world of consumption. Sure, plenty of people know about quinoa, but why exactly is it healthy?

A Substitute for Less Healthy Foods

Quinoa is quite a versatile little food, and it can be used in place of many other foods that are not quite as healthy. For example, instead of serving rice or pasta, you could cook quinoa in a similar manner and still have a delicious meal. Sauces, seasonings and light butter all work well with quinoa just as they do with the less healthy options.

Eating Quinoa in Place of Beef

Unless you choose the leanest cuts of beef, you are almost always consuming more fat and calories than when you choose chicken, fish or a vegetable dish. What are you supposed to put in the tacos and burritos though, and how will you ever have burgers again? When mixed with a binding agent, quinoa becomes the perfect substance to replace burgers. You can add in some cheese, lettuce or your other favorite burger mixing Ingredients ; you could even make a quinoa loaf! As for Mexican dishes, you can use quinoa in instead of beef.

It's a Whole Grain

White breads, flours and pastas really bring the pounds onto your body, but whole grains do not have the same effect. Not only do white breads and the like make you gain more weight, but they also are not suitable options for people who are gluten free. Due to dieting trends and an increase of various medical conditions, more people are looking to eat gluten free but cannot find enough choices. Fortunately for them, quinoa is one food that is free of this substance.

It Contains Plenty of Necessary Nutrients

Now, eating healthy is not all about avoiding foods that make you gain weight;

it's also about finding dishes that have the necessary nutrients that you need. According to the Food Network, quinoa contains iron, vitamin B6, zinc, folate, thiamin, potassium, selenium and magnesium. It seems that no matter what nutrient you are lacking, quinoa is there to help make up the difference. Quinoa will help to provide you with the necessary energy and body building agents that can help you get through the day and function to the best of your abilities.

The Nutritional Components

When it comes to health, everyone is very concerned about the amount of calories and such that they are putting into their bodies. When it comes to quinoa, the Food Network is able to report exciting information about these numbers as well. A full cup of quinoa, once it has been cooked, has 220 calories, eight grams of protein and five grams of fiber. If you are a little bit concerned about the calories, don't worry. Quinoa is a very filling substance, and, if you are having it as a side dish, it's unlikely that you would be able to eat an entire cup.

. . .

It Can Curb Your Appetite

As noted earlier, quinoa is an extremely filling food. When it's in the package, it might not look as though it is so. However, once you cook quinoa, it really fluffs out. The texture also makes it suitable for chewing, so you don't just inhale it all up. If you are having a serving of quinoa with your lunch or dinner, it might fill you up so that you do not wind up eating an excessive amount of healthy food. After eating a dinner with quinoa, you likely will not be tempted to reach for that tub of ice cream either.

Eating More Slowly

When it comes to any sort of grainy substance, you're going to usually have to eat more slowly. It's not as though you are eating a slice of steak or taking a bite out of a burger. Quinoa requires some time to eat, and this will let you fill up at a more normal pace. When you gobble through food, your body often does not realize that it is full until you have consumed way too much food for your body to handle without putting on weight.

Protecting Against Certain Diseases

Another of the health benefits of quinoa is that it can actually help to protect your body against certain types of diseases. According to the World's Healthiest Foods, the nutritional benefits of quinoa can help you avoid medical issues such as diabetes. While conclusive evidence has not been shown, it is true that many of the nutrients in quinoa have been associated with an increased risk of this disease. Furthermore, this site also reports that quinoa can help to reduce cholesterol. It's also necessary to point out that quinoa can have some secondary positive effects on your health as well. Essentially, as we have seen, quinoa is likely to help lower your chances of becoming overweight or obese. Being overweight or obese can increase your risk of other types of diseases, so quinoa helps to protect against them as well.

It is probably quite difficult to make an argument against the health benefits of quinoa after reading through all of this information. One of the other positive notes about quinoa is that it actually tastes good, and it does work very well as a substitute in many foods. You can enjoy the health benefits and the taste at the same time.

POPULAR VEGAN RECIPES THAT USE QUINOA

Whether you are indulging in quinoa for the first time or just looking for new recipes, these vegan dishes will satisfy your craving for the nutritious grain.

1
QUINOA AND BLACK BEANS

Ingredients

- 1 teaspoon vegetable oil
- ½ cup chopped fresh cilantro

- 1 chopped onion
- 30 ounces of black beans, drained and rinsed 3 cloves peeled and chopped garlic

- 1 cup frozen corn kernels
- ¾ cup uncooked quinoa
- ¼ teaspoon cayenne pepper 1 ½ cups vegetable broth Pepper and salt to taste

- 1 teaspoon ground cumin

Directions

In a medium saucepan, warm the oil on a medium flame. Add the garlic and onion, and sauté until just browned.

Mix the quinoa in the same saucepan, and then pour the vegetable broth over the mixture. Season with pepper, cumin, salt and cayenne pepper then boil the mixture. Reduce heat and simmer covered for 20 minutes.

Sir in the frozen corn, then simmer for five additional minutes until the mixture is heated through. Add the cilantro and black beans then serve.

2

LEMON AND SPINACH QUINOA BAKE

Ingredients

3 cups vegetable broth
   2 tablespoons nutritional yeast

1 cup quinoa
   ¼ teaspoon black pepper 1 tablespoon olive oil
   1 teaspoon fresh lemon zest 2 teaspoons egg replacer

4 tablespoons of water

1 cup tofu sour cream
1 medium onion, diced

1 pound spinach leaves
2 cloves garlic, minced
¼ teaspoon red-pepper flakes

1 tablespoon fresh thyme leaves
1 tablespoon fresh rosemary, chopped Directions

Boil the quinoa and vegetable broth. Let simmer for 20 minutes or until fluffy.

Preheat the oven to 350 degrees, and then brush a ceramic baking dish with olive oil.

Whisk the water and egg replacer together in a large bowl then set aside.

In a medium pan, heat one tablespoon of olive oil. Add the garlic and onion and sauté for eight minutes.

Add the rosemary, red-pepper flakes, spinach and thyme. Sauté until wilted, then transfer it to the egg mixture.

Add the sour cream, pepper, nutritional yeast, lemon zest and quinoa to the spinach mixture. Stir until combined, then pour into the prepared dish and bake for 60 minutes. Let cool before slicing, then serve warm.

3
QUINOA-GNOCCHI POTATO SALAD

Ingredients for Salad

- ½ cup quinoa
- ¼ cup fresh dill

Popular Vegan Recipes That Use Quinoa

- 500 grams vegan gnocchi
- 1/3 cup green onions, sliced

- 2 cups green beans
- Ingredients

- **for Dressing**
- 1/3 cup extra-virgin olive oil
- ¼ teaspoon salt
- 1 tablespoon vegan mayonnaise 1 minced garlic clove

- 1 tablespoon Dijon mustard

Directions

Whisk together the dressing Ingredients in a large bowl, then set aside.

1. Bring the quinoa to a boil, then simmer covered for 20 minutes.

1. In a separate pot, boil the gnocchi for 2 to 3 minutes.

Drain the gnocchi using a slotted spoon and add them to the bowl containing the dressing.

1. In the same water used to boil the gnocchi, cook the green beans for about 5 minutes until they are tender yet crisp. Drain the beans then mix them with the gnocchi and dressing.

1. Add the cooked quinoa, then top with the dill and green onions and serve.

4

QUINOA SALAD WITH BLACK AND WHITE BEANS

Ingredients for Salad 1/3 cup quinoa

- ¼ chopped fresh cilantro
- 1 can black beans, rinsed and drained

- 1 seeded and minced jalapeno pepper
- ¼ cup diced red onion
- 1 can rinsed and drained navy beans

- cup diced cucumbers

Ingredients for Dressing

- ¼ cup vegetable or olive oil
- ¼ teaspoon pepper

- 2tablespoons lime juice
- ¼ teaspoon salt

- 1 tablespoon apple cider vinegar
- ½ teaspoon dried oregano 1 clove garlic, minced
- 1 teaspoon ground coriander

- 1 teaspoon chili powder

Popular Vegan Recipes That Use Quinoa

Directions

1. Cook the quinoa for about 12 minutes or until tender in boiling salted water. Drain, rinse and set aside.

1. In a separate large bowl, whisk together the dressing ingredients. Add the remaining salad Ingredients and the quinoa. Toss and serve.

1. Quinoa Chili

1. Ingredients

1. 1 cup corn kernels

1. cup quinoa
2. Salt and pepper to taste

1. cups vegetable stock
2. ½ teaspoon ground cumin

1. 1 tablespoon olive oil
2. ½ teaspoon dried oregano 1 large onion, diced

1. teaspoon chili powder
2. cloves garlic, minced
3. cans kidney beans (do not drain) 2 stalks diced celery
4. cans diced tomatoes with juices

1. 1 peeled and diced carrot
2. 1 seeded and diced red bell pepper
3. Optional: tortilla chips, cucumber, vegan sour cream, avocado and cilantro

Directions

1. In a medium saucepan, boil the vegetable stock. Add the quinoa and simmer for about 15 minutes. Set aside.

1. Over medium heat in a large saucepan, heat the olive oil. Add the garlic and onions. Sauté for about 3 minutes, (until tender) then add the celery and carrot and continue sautéing for about 3 minutes. Add the salt, pepper, tomatoes, bell pepper, oregano, kidney beans and chili powder. Bring to a boil then simmer for 30 minutes uncovered. Stir occasionally, and then add the corn and quinoa.

1. Add the optional Ingredients if desired, then serve warm.

5

TROPICAL BREAKFAST QUINOA

Ingredients

- 1 tablespoon desiccated coconut
- ¾ cups water or soy milk
- ¼ cup fresh pineapple

- 1/3 cup of quinoa flakes and oatmeal blended together Directions
- Spread the coconut on a baking sheet and bake for 20 minutes at 300 degrees. Stir frequently to ensure the coconut evenly browns. Alternatively, you can brown the coconut on the stove top in a small skillet. Cook over medium heat, stirring often.
- While the coconut is browning, cook the quinoa and oatmeal blend with the water or soy milk for 1.5 minutes in the microwave. Top with the toasted coconut and fresh pineapple.

POPULAR CHICKEN RECIPES THAT USE QUINOA

6

YUMMY CHICKEN BURRITOS

This recipe is a quick and easy recipe that your whole family will love. In addition to tasting great, these chicken burritos have plenty of protein, whole grains and vitamins.

Ingredients:

- Four large to extra large whole grain tortillas

- tablespoons of cilantro
- One cup of dry quinoa

- 2 cups cubed and cooked chicken breast Lettuce
- Four tablespoons of mayo
- ½ cup cubed tomatoes

Directions:

Step one: The first step is to cook the quinoa. In a pot, add one cup of dry quinoa and two cups of water. If desired, salt the water with ¼ tsp of salt and pepper. Cook until the quinoa is fluffy.

Step two: Gather your tortillas, and heat them for 15 seconds in the microwave. Once the tortillas are warm, not crispy, add the lettuce and tomatoes. Next, add one tablespoon of cilantro for every tortilla. Afterwards, add a few tablespoons of quinoa to the tortilla, but make sure you don't add too much. After you add the quinoa, add ½ cup chicken in every tortilla. Then, the final step is to add the mayonnaise and fold the tortilla to give it its shape.

7

QUINOA STIR FRY

This dish has oriental roots, and it's packed with plenty of good-for-you veggies. In addition, this dish is quick and easy to make, and it doesn't take more than 30 minutes to prepare.

Ingredients:

- 2 cup of dry quinoa
- Four skinless chicken breasts

- 2 large carrots
- Green onions

- Red onions Cilantro Soy sauce
- ½ of a red and green bell pepper Butter

Directions:

1. Step one: The first step for making this dish to cook the quinoa. In a pot, add 2 cups of quinoa with four cups of water. Next, add salt and pepper to the water. Once most of the water evaporates, put a lid on the pot and turn down the heat to medium/ low.

1. Step two: Gather the chicken, and then make sure to wash it thoroughly. Season the chicken on both sides with salt and pepper. In a skillet or grill, cook the chicken thoroughly.

1. Step three: Cut all of your vegetables into small pieces. In a skillet, add the butter and onions together; cook them until the onion is golden brown. Once the onion

is golden, you need to add the rest of the vegetables into the skillet except the cilantro. Add the soy sauce, and stir the mixture together. Once you add the soy sauce, add the chicken and quinoa. Fold the stir fry over until the Ingredients are blended together.

8

GREEK PITA

This recipe is a fresh take on a classic dish; the mayonnaise is a yummy surprise no one will expect. In addition, this recipe is perfect for an on-the-go person, and it's a great lunch box recipe for school lunches.

Ingredients:

Popular Chicken Recipes that Use Quinoa

- Four pita pockets
- ½ cup mayo
- Cooked chicken breasts
- ½ cup cooked green grapes Cilantro to garnish
- Cubed tomatoes

Directions:

- Step one: First, cut the grapes in half. Next, gather the chicken breasts and cut them into cubs. After you cut the chicken, get a bowl and add the chicken, grapes, tomatoes and cilantro. Mix the Ingredients until they are perfectly incorporated. Once you mix the ingredients, add the mayo. Then, fill the pita pockets with the mix you made, and enjoy.

9

MEXICAN FIESTA

This recipe is perfect for people who love spicy foods because it packs a punch of hot flavors. Plus, the colors in this dish will make everyone melt, and their taste buds will swoon.

Ingredients:

- Four cooked chicken breasts Hot sauce
- cups chicken broth

Popular Chicken Recipes that Use Quinoa

- 1 chopped red bell pepper
- jalapeno pepper; finely chopped
- ¼ tsp chili powder

- cups quinoa

Directions:

1. Step one: In a pot, add the chicken broth, chili powder and the quinoa; cook them until the quinoa becomes fluffy.

1. Step two: Slice the chicken into fajita-like slices, and cut the pepper in fajita-like slices, too.

1. Step three: In a large serving dish, add all of the quinoa; then, top it off with the vegetables and chicken. Enjoy.

10

QUESADILLA

This is a yummy recipe that kids will adore because of all the gooey cheese. Mothers and fathers will love this recipe too because it is loaded with calcium, whole grains, fiber and vitamins.

Ingredients: 1 cup quinoa

Popular Chicken Recipes that Use Quinoa

. . .

2 cups chicken broth
 ½ shredded American cheese and ½ mozzarella cheese

4 large tortillas
 Cubed cooked chicken

Cilantro Salsa
 Jalapeno; optional Directions:
Step One: In a pot, cook the quinoa with the chicken broth. Cook it until the quinoa is fluffy.

Step two: Gather the tortilla, and fill it with chicken, quinoa, peppers, tomatoes and a lot of cheese. Cook the quesadillas until the cheese melts completely; serve.

11

QUINOA AND BEANS

This recipe is very delicious and very hearty. The chicken complements the quinoa and beans perfectly, so everyone will love this dish. Plus, it has plenty of nutrition such as: vitamins, minerals, protein, healthy fats and carbs.

Ingredients:
   4 cooked chicken breasts 2 cups quinoa
   2 cups beans
   Salt and pepper
   Butter

Popular Chicken Recipes that Use Quinoa

Step one: In a pot, cook the quinoa with four cups of water, salt and pepper until it is fluffy. Once the Quinoa cooks get a skillet with butter and add the chicken. Then, add the beans with the chicken and stir. Add the quinoa and blend the Ingredients together. Serve with cilantro on top for added flavor.

POPULAR BEEF RECIPES THAT USE QUINOA

Quinoa is becoming a popular addition in the food industry. It is being used in various cooking where it allows you to be creative without feeling guilty. Since quinoa is great source of protein and gluten-free grain, the nutritional value is increased. Quinoa is mostly used in salads; however, it is so versatile that it is used in a lot of different dishes. Here we will discuss adding Quinoa with popular beef recipes.

Grilled Beef Tenderloin is an interesting dish that allows you to experience this style of preparation that will be pleasing to the pallet. This recipe uses quinoa and beef in an interesting way.

12

GRILLED BEEF TENDERLOIN WITH LEEK TOMATO QUINOA AND ROASTED GARLIC SAUCE

For Sauce-While preparing the sauce, you should preheat the oven at 350 degrees Fahrenheit. Together with two cups of whole milk and two large heads of garlic (1/3 trimmed) you would add them in a small saucepan. You would leave saucepan uncovered with medium heat for ten minutes. Doing this allows it to simmer. Once done after ten minutes, drain milk and put garlic in an ovenproof dish small in size. There you would pour half cup of olive oil over it and let it cool. Ensure dish is covered tightly with regular foil.

. . .

In the oven let garlic bake for 55 minutes or until soft. Then, spoon garlic out from dish and pour olive oil into a measuring cup; if you required more oil add as necessary to measure at ½ a cup total. Remove peel from garlic and put into blender. You are going to add ½ cup of low-salt chicken broth, garlic, and olive oil. Then puree until smooth, you may thin with more broth as you desire. Add salt and pepper to season. For Beef-Barbecue grill is turned to medium heat. Brush oil over beef and lightly shake salt and pepper to season. Place beef on warm grill and let it grill to desired doneness (it is good to turn it often to allow both sides to grill). Do this for about twenty-two minutes for a medium-rare finish. Let it stand for five minutes after removing from grill. Then, slice crosswise at 1/3 inch thick slices.

13

LEEK-TOMATO QUINOA

Rinse one and a half cup of quinoa with cold water using mesh filter if necessary until the water is clear. Add quinoa in two cups of water and half teaspoon of salt in medium-sized saucepan heavy in weight. Let it come to a boil and reduce heat by medium-low. Cover saucepan to let it simmer until quinoa is tender or water is absorbed, which takes about 20 minutes. Then drain quinoa and set it aside (you can prepare this the day before). Let one tablespoon of butter melt in a warm large nonstick skillet over medium heat.

Sauté two cups of chopped leeks for about five minutes (until almost soft) then pour chicken broth and let it simmer until leeks are soft (five minutes). Add quinoa and three tablespoons of olive oil then stir for about five minutes. Then, add chopped (2 medium-sized with seeds removed) yellow tomatoes, three tablespoon of chopped leeks, three tablespoon of chopped fresh basil, and one tablespoon of fresh lemon juice (squeezed from fresh lemons) and stir for five minutes. Add ½ teaspoon of salt and pepper to season.

Spoon the Leek-Tomato Quinoa onto four plates then add grilled tenderloin beef, sauce and chives over it.

14

BEEF STIR FRY WITH QUINOA

This is a popular meal that is usually straight forward and not time consuming. Vegetables and grains make cooking interesting because it adds a new twist to a rather simple dish. Here you add another nutrition that will make your meals leaner with protein.

This recipe allows you to enjoy eating a nutritious gluten-free grain with your favorite meat item, beef. Beef stir-fry w/Quinoa. All vegetables are pre-cut or diced and the beef is pre-cut for stir-fry. Heat frying pan in medium heat, add half cup of sesame oil (for cooking). When sesame oil is warm, add strips of beef and stir as it cooks and starts to brown. Add ½ cup chopped three cloves of garlic (pre-peeled) and ½ cup of chopped onions. Then stir with beef strips. Include one cup of frozen peas and carrots, ½ cup chopped bell peppers, and add one cup of green onions.

Stir together with the beef and add three tablespoons of marinade for added specific flavor (or to taste). Allow stir-fry to cook thoroughly, for about ten- fifteen minutes. Prepare Quinoa: rinse one cup of quinoa in strainer with two cups of cold water until the water runs clear. Cook quinoa in regular saucepan for about twenty minutes or until water is absorbed. Set aside.

In separate plate, spoon in generous amount of quinoa and top it off with beef and vegetable stir fry. This would make about 2-3 serving sizes.

Cooked quinoa has zero cholesterol, eight grams of protein, four grams of total fat, thirty-nine grams of carbohydrates, thirteen grams of sodium, zero sugars, five grams of dietary fiber, and calories total two-hundred twenty-two. This is based on one cup serving size.

POPULAR SEAFOOD RECIPES THAT USE QUINOA

15

SALAD QUINOA SEAFOOD

Ingredients

1 ½ cups of assorted frozen seafood

1 cup of cooked quinoa
    ½ cup of sliced cucumber

1 diced tomato
    ½ cup of diced yellow or orange bell pepper
    ¼ of a cup onion
    ¼ cup of crumbled feta cheese
    ¼ cup of black olives
    2 tablespoons of olive oil
    1 tablespoon of lemon juice

. . .

PAMELA KENDRICK

1 garlic clove crushed
    Salt and pepper to taste

2 cups of baby spinach

Directions

If you are not starting with cooked quinoa, then prepare quinoa as per Directions
    on the package to get one cup of cooked quinoa.

Bring some water to boil, and cook the frozen seafood until it has completely thawed out and has heated all the way through. Make sure the seafood is completely submerged in the boiling water.

Once the quinoa and seafood has cooled to room temperature, add in the cucumbers, tomatoes, onions, olives, bell peppers and feta cheese and gently mix it all together.

Put the olive oil, lemon juice, garlic, oregano, salt and pepper in to a jar, and shake it until it is well mixed up and drizzle over the salad.

Place salad in refrigerated until you are ready to serve.

Just before serving, roughly chop the baby spinach and add to the salad. Give it one last gentle mix and serve.

. . .

This salad tastes delicious after it has been refrigerated for several hours. It is great to make in the morning and have for lunch or dinner.

16

SALMON QUINOA CAKES

Ingredients

3 cans of unsalted salmon
½ cup of dry quinoa
1 bunch of green onions
1 tablespoon of minced fresh dill 1 tablespoon of lemon zest
1 tablespoon of olive oil

1 large egg
    Salt and pepper to taste

Directions

Bring one cup of water to boil and add the quinoa. Cover and let it sit until the water has been completely absorbed. This takes about 10 minutes. When it is cooked, take off the top so it can cool down to room temperature.

Prepare the salmon by deboning it and removing the skin. Place it in to a large bowl and break it in to small pieces with a fork.

Place the dill, onions, lemon zest and salt and pepper in to the food processor. Process for about 4 to 5 seconds, or until the onion is finely minced.

Once the quinoa has cooled, add it to the food processor with the salmon.

Process until it has all come together to form a dough. This takes about 10 seconds.

Crack the egg in to a bowl and add the salmon and quinoa mixture form the food processor. Mix with a large spoon until it all comes together.

Form the quinoa salmon mixture in to flat cakes like a burger. Heat olive oil in a nonstick pan or in a cast iron skillet and fry each cake until it is golden brown. This takes about three minutes on each side.

Serve with your favorite buns and toppings or as a side dish with fries and salad.

17

QUINOA WITH ROASTED FISH AND VEGGIES

Ingredients

1 ½ cups of grape tomatoes

2carrots cut in to sticks
 1 large yellow bell pepper cut in to wide strips 1 medium to small onion cut in to thin slices
 3cloves of garlic, crushed
 4pieces of fish, flounder or tilapia work well, each pieces should be about 3 ounces
 Zest and juice of 1 lemon Salt

PAMELA KENDRICK

. . .

1 cup of dry quinoa
   3 tablespoons of toasted pine nuts to garnish Directions
   Cook quinoa according to the Directions
   on the package. Preheat oven to 400°F.
   Line a 9 by 13 inch pan with parchment paper.

Place carrots, tomatoes, bell pepper, onion, garlic in the pan and sprinkle with salt. This assortment of vegetables can be changed to your liking. Adding zucchini and fresh green beans are another option.

Bake the vegetables until they are tender, about 25 minutes.

Take vegetables out of the oven and stir. Add the fish and top with lemon juice and zest. Sprinkle the fish with salt, and put it back in the oven until the fish is cooked, about another 20 minutes.

Serve vegetables and fish on top of quinoa and garnish with pine nuts.

Shrimp and Quinoa Croquettes with Sauce

Ingredients

2 cups of cooked quinoa 1 cup of raw shrimp

. . .

2 eggs
¼ cup of onion, finely chopped

1 teaspoon of salt
1½ teaspoons of grated fresh ginger Ingredients for dipping sauce:
½ cup of soy sauce

2 tablespoons of white vinegar
¾ of a cup of water
1 green chili chopped up very small or a teaspoon of red chili sauce (optional) Directions for Sauce

In a small serving bowl, mix all the Ingredients and let it sit for at least 10 minutes before serving.

Alternatively, you can make one bowl of sauce plain and the other spicy. Directions for Croquettes

If you are starting with uncooked quinoa, then cook as per directions on the package.

In a large bowl, beat the eggs until they are well mixed. Chop the shrimp in to small bits and add to egg mixture.

Add the finely chopped onions, ginger and salt. Mix together until all Ingredients have combined and it is possible to make it in to balls.

Heat up rice bran or canola oil in a deep frying pan. Once the oil has heated up, keep it on medium heat. If it is too hot, then they will burn on the outside and be raw inside.

. . .

Add the quinoa and shrimp balls in to the oil and cook until they are golden brown.

Take them out of the oil, and place them on a paper towel for a couple of minutes to absurd some of the oil.

Serve with dipping sauce.

POPULAR PORK (OR LAMB) RECIPES THAT USE QUINOA

18

PORK (OR LAMB) FRIED QUINOA

1 1/2 cups quinoa
2 1/4 cups cold water - add a dash of salt 1 tbsp neutral oil - canola or vegetable
1 1/2 cups diced ham - diced 3/4 cup green onions - sliced
3/4 cup green pepper - diced (substitute with red or yellow peppers) 3 cloves garlic - minced

1 tbsp rice vinegar
Soy sauce to taste or 1 to 2 tbsp Hot sauce to taste

Garnish with toasted sesame seeds and
Rinse quinoa thoroughly under cold water and add to

saucepan. Add cold water. Stir, cover and bring to a simmer for about 15 minutes. Turn off heat, set aside and fluff finished.

Prep vegetables while quinoa is cooking. Add oil, ham, green onions and peppers to a frying pan over medium heat. Cook while stirring for 3 to 4 minutes. The ham should be slightly caramelized with the onions. Turn off the heat and brown the garlic.

Add fluffed quinoa to the frying pan. Stir together over medium heat for 2 minutes.

Add rice vinegar and soy sauce or hot sauce to taste. Serve hot and garnish with toasted sesame seeds.

19

PORK TENDERLOIN WITH QUINOA PILAF

Ingredients:
   2 pork tenderloins - 1.25 lbs 2 tbsp olive oil
   2 egg whites - beaten
   1 tbsp fresh rosemary - chopped 1 tbsp fresh sage - chopped
   1 tbsp fresh thyme - chopped 1 tsp salt

1tsp black pepper
   Add salt to tenderloins.

. . .

Heat oil in a large skillet over medium-high for 2 minutes then add tenderloins. Cook each side for 2 minutes until browned. Set aside to cool.

Preheat oven to 350 degrees.

Brush tenderloin on all sides with egg white.

On wax paper or a plate, mix together the rosemary, sage, thyme, salt and pepper. Roll the pork through the mixture.

Place a wire rack on a sheet pan and put the pork on top of it. Place the sheet pan in the oven.

Bake 20 minutes or until the pork achieves a 145 degree internal temperature.

Remove pork from oven and let it stand for 10 minutes. Slice and serve with quinoa.

20

PORK QUINOA SOUP

Ingredients:

    2 tablespoons of olive oil

    1 teaspoon ground annatto seed (substitute with sweet paprika)
1 cup leek - diced (white part and 1-inch of the green)

    1/2 cup scallions - diced (use the white part and little of the green - 1 inch) 1/2 teaspoon cumin (ground)

    5 garlic cloves - create a paste with 1/2 tsp pepper & 1 tsp salt
1 medium tomato - chopped and peeled - about 6 oz

    3/4 lb lean pork - trim fat and cut into 1/2-inch cubes

. . .

6 cups hot water
    3/4 cup cooked quinoa (instructions below)
    1 lb peeled waxy potatoes - cut into 1-inch cubes

1 cup of milk
    1/4 cup natural peanut butter (substitute with 1/4 cup unsalted dry roasted peanuts)
    7 large fresh basil leaves - chopped Cayenne pepper to taste - or 1 pinch

1 cup of peas - frozen
    Garnish with fresh minced parsley

Use a 4-quart saucepan to heat the olive oil over low heat. Stir in the annatto until dispersed. Add the leeks, scallions, cumin and garlic paste. Cook for 5 minutes, mixing often.

Turn the heat to medium and add the pork. Cook for 2 minutes and mix well with previous ingredients.

Add water and allow contents come to a boil. Turn down the heat down and leave to simmer for 40 to 50 minutes.

While that's simmering, cook the quinoa.

Rinse quinoa under cold water for a few seconds. Bring 1 1/3 cups of water to a boil. Stir in quinoa, cover pot and let simmer for approximately ten minutes or until water is absorbed. Remove from heat and set aside after cooked.

Popular Pork (or Lamb) Recipes That Use Quinoa

. . .

Purée milk and peanut butter then set purée mixture aside.

Add quinoa, potatoes and purée mixture. Cook about 20 minutes until potatoes tenderize.

Add the basil, cayenne and peas. Cook 2 minutes while stirring. Add seasoning to taste and garnish with parsley. Serve at once.

21

QUINOA AND HAM OMELETS

Ingredients:
  Two eggs

1 tsp vegetable oil
   1/3 cup ham
   1/4 cup green onions 1/4 cup green pepper 1/4 cup cooked quinoa Salt to taste
   Pepper to taste

. . .

Popular Pork (or Lamb) Recipes That Use Quinoa

Whisk eggs until frothy. Add oil to skillet and heat for 2 minutes. Add egg mixture to skillet. Cook for 3 minutes over medium heat.

Add ham, green onions, green pepper, salt, pepper and quinoa. Cook until egg is easily loosened from the side with a spatula. Fold the omelet in half and serve hot.

2

GLUTEN FREE

A Healthier Diet

Gluten Free diets are typically entered into by necessity, not by chance. That doesn't mean, however, that there are no real benefits to making the choice to go gluten free. In fact, for those who are considering a diet that may help to lower their cholesterol and make other positive, long-term health changes, going gluten free has some potential health benefits that may not have been considered.

Going gluten free has become a fairly popular new trend. You might even consider it to be one of those diet "fads" that hit the magazine and book shelves every few years. The difference is that most fads are not healthy and really don't help a great deal. This fad--which is not really a fad--is being seen to increase the energy and to improve the overall good health of many people who use it.

. . .

Celebrities such as Gwyneth Paltrow and Chelsea Clinton are finding that gluten free works for them, and it can work for you too. It's quite likely that you're seeing more and more gluten free products hitting the supermarket shelves recently. For those who have no food allergies and aren't concerned with gluten in their diet, going gluten free is something you probably haven't explored very carefully. The reason for the growing number of gluten free foods is that many people have explored gluten free and found that even if they don't' have to utilize the diet, it's much healthier--quite like the paleo diets which are so popular.

What is Gluten?

Gluten is a kind of protein that is part of grains and cereal products such as wheat. It tends To make bread and foods elastic, or chewy tasting. It keeps food from being "sticky." Gluten is found in flour products of wheat, but more, it is also found in other grains.

There are such a wide range of people who have a problem with gluten that it is considered to be one of the big 8 which are mandated to be listed on food packaging. If you have a gluten intolerance or allergy, going gluten free for you

isn't a choice, it's a necessity and you need To make sure that you don't accidentally take in gluten in some form by mistake.

Become an expert at reading the packaging and finding out precisely what is in the product and not just that, what it has come into contact with so that you know your products are gluten free.

People who have certain food allergies or disease processes such as Celiac disease may not be able to tolerate even a tiny amount of gluten in their diet. One of the most common questions to be found among those who are newly diagnosed with Celiac is what they can and cannot eat. Take that a step further and realize that not only edible products have gluten, but many inedible ones do as well. Be very careful to wash your hands after using some soaps, lotions and even pet foods as these have nominal amounts of gluten in them which could be transferred to your food if you don't wash carefully after using them.

Advantages of Going Gluten Free.

Doctors and naturalists have taken a good look at gluten free diets recently and found that gluten free can help to improve the overall good health of even those who are not suffering from a gluten allergy.

It can help to improve your serum cholesterol level, may also promote better digestion, and might even increase your energy, particularly if you may be suffering from a gluten allergy or intolerance. The reason for this is not that gluten itself is particularly unhealthy. Many of the foods which are made from gluten or with gluten incorporated into them tend to be less healthy than those which do not contain it.

Gluten Free Cooking

Gluten free foods impose some big challenges. It makes it hard to enjoy foods that you may have eaten your entire life, but with a little work, you can make those recipes your own and in many cases, you'll be surprised at what foods are
 out there are naturally gluten free.

. . .

For example, a vanilla milkshake made with all natural ice cream is normally gluten free. Fresh strawberries, spinach, fruits of nearly all types and vegetables are gluten free naturally.

Even many of your favorite snack foods will be gluten free. Potato chips and most corn chips which are fried or baked in corn oil or soybean oil are gluten free. Check the packaging, but most are baked or fried using heart healthy methods and so are gluten free without any help from you. While these are not the ideal snacks, they are able to be eaten in moderation.

While it may be moderately frustrating at first trying to replace things like cake flour and find ways To make pasta and cookies, the more you look at gluten free meals, the more you'll find that you can create nearly any recipe that you like with gluten free foods and emulate most any recipe that you'll find with common sense and a bit of skill in substitution.

Take a look your new diet and approach it with the attitude of exploring new things, a challenge rather than a chore and you'll find that in no time, you and your family have really conquered the world of gluten free cooking. You may even find that you enjoy cooking more and that eating is more fun, better tasting, and healthier by far than those which incorporate the very sticky gluten filled processed foods that you were accustomed to.

Which Foods Would Be Eliminated in a Gluten Free Diet?

In many cases, the foods which are not healthy for you anyway, particularly processed foods would be missing from your diet.

Foods such as white bread, white crackers and other processed wheat products are going to be eliminated from your diet. Noodles of many types are foods which won't be allowed to be eaten, but they can be replaced with rice noodles and other forms of pasta which are healthy and tasty.

The problem is that many people like the taste of these foods, and don't consider the many unhealthy components that are part of them. Foods which are processed such as supermarket breads and pastries contain not just gluten, but unhealthy fats, many preservatives, and other chemicals that are higher in
   disease promoting ingredients.

What Makes Gluten Free a Good Choice?

Studies show that eating a low gluten or gluten free diet can lower your risk of some disease processes such as heart disease, certain types of cancer, type 2 diabetes, and many other long term health conditions. Your diet would be richer in fruits and vegetables and would quite likely contain many more foods that offer positive health benefits and a higher level of vitamins, phytonutrients, and antioxidants.

Making Gluten-Free Work for You

Every year more and more people are diagnosed with celiac disease. They are required to eat a gluten free diet. You perhaps are not required to go gluten free, but the health benefits of doing so are nothing short of amazing. Even if you do not have celiac disease or an allergy to gluten which compels you to avoid oats, wheat, rye and malt, if you follow the gluten free diet even loosely, you may find that you feel better, that your skin is much clearer, and that you may have a lower incidence of heartburn, fatigue, and cramping.

The poor vitamin absorption that takes place in Celiac disease can make the person who suffers from this disease feel very unwell, have side effects of loose stool and even depression. It is imperative to stay within the dietary restrictions which have been given to you and to understand why you have those restrictions.

Basing your diet on a gluten free approach may be a good idea, but for the Celiac sufferer, it's something that is non-optional. The very strict limitations that apply to the celiac sufferer would not apply to those who are making a choice to go gluten-free, but sticking as closely as you can to the gluten-free approach will improve your health by removing most of the high fats and fried foods that we should quite likely be avoiding anyway. It can be a genuinely healthy way to eat, improving your serum cholesterol and your energy. It's not necessary to be as strict with yourself, such as avoiding malt flavors, when you
are not genuinely restricted, but staying close to the diet so far as main meal ingredients will be beneficial for your entire family.

Gluten Intolerance and Allergies

Today for whatever reason, many people are actively allergic to gluten, to wheat and to other components of wheat. The numbers of these people grow continuously every year. It is particularly difficult in the case of children to limit gluten in the diet. If their allergic reaction is bad enough, the reaction can be devastating and foods which have gluten must be completely eliminated. Using rice noodles and gluten free foods is an imperative, not a choice. In addition, some diseases exist which require that people who suffer from them do not have gluten of any type as part of their diet. This means that not only wheat, but other foods which contain gluten must be eliminated from the diet.

Celiac is a serious illness with real consequences if the sufferer does not eliminate gluten. Keep in mind that making the choice to go gluten free means that you can be a little more lenient with yourself. You may eat foods such as soy sauce and other things that are not available to the sufferer of celiac or gluten intolerance. To that end, our book contains only recipes that are strictly and completely gluten free in order to be useful to the user who has chosen to go gluten free, as well as to the celiac client, who has a need to follow a strict gluten free method of eating.

What Are You Giving Up?

One of the first comments that people make when considering a gluten free diet is that they won't be able to enjoy desserts and other things that they are accustomed to and simply want on an occasional basis. The fact is that some things will be off limits, specifically processed pastries and that type of foods. That doesn't mean that there is nothing to replace it.

Eliminating gluten from your diet does not mean sacrificing taste. In fact, quite the opposite. Many of the things that you eat on a gluten free diet will be sweet
    treats that you make yourself. They won't incorporate high fat and gluten, of course, but they will incorporate fresh fruits, even cocoa in some cases, so you won't lose your chocolate or some of the other foods that you love. They can be eaten sparingly and

when created with the correct ingredients don't add gluten or even a high amount of empty calories to your meals.

Gluten Free foods don't have to be lacking in taste or fiber. Here are some wonderful examples of what can be done with gluten free cooking, listed for you in sections.

MAIN DISH GLUTEN FREE RECIPES.

Main dish recipes are one of the most difficult to accomplish without any gluten but with a little imagination and creativity, you can come up with some wonderful meals that are gluten free and have incredible taste and appeal. Some perfect examples of gluten free main dish recipes include these, which are all created for the person who really has to have no gluten at all incorporated into their diet.

22

LAMB WITH YAMS AND APPLES

This is completely gluten free and offers great taste as well as ample nutrition. The pairing of apples and yams offers a little sweetness to the pork as well as keeping it moist.

You will need:

. . .

PAMELA KENDRICK

1/4 cup dark brown sugar

5 tablespoons butter, melted 1 tsp vinegar
   1tsp salt

1/2 tsp granulated garlic 2 apples, cored and sliced
   2sweet potatoes, peeled and sliced

2 chops, preferably the tenderloin style
   To make:

Preheat oven to 400 degrees Fahrenheit.

Mix the sugar, the butter the vinegar and the spices.

Keep about a tablespoon of the butter mix and set it aside.

Add the apple and sweet potato to your brown sugar mix and coat them.
   Place the apples and potatoes in a roasting pan and cover with foil. Bake for twenty minutes.

Meanwhile lightly brown the lamb in the remaining butter mix.

Remove the potato and apple mixture from the oven and add the lamb over the top of the mix.

. . .

Replace the dish in the oven and bake it for approximately 40 minutes until a meat thermometer shows that the lamb is cooked.

23

CHEESY MEXICAN CHICKEN

Cheesy chicken becomes an instant favorite when you create it combined with cheese. Low in fat and high in nutrients, chicken is a favorite food for about half the world. This has a bit of a bite to it, with the chili peppers and tomato added

You will need:
 2 tablespoon of olive oil 1 can diced tomatoes 1/2 teaspoon sea salt fresh ground pepper
 1/2 cup finely chopped green onion 1 chopped clove of garlic
 1 tsp chopped fresh cilantro 1 can diced green chilies

Main Dish Gluten Free Recipes.

1 can black beans

1/3 cup Colby jack cheese 2 cups cooked white rice

To make:

Chop the chicken into cubes and brown in the olive oil, sprinkling with the sea salt and pepper.

Add the remaining ingredients, excluding the cheese.
 Allow to cook on the stove top on low heat for approximately 40 minutes, until chicken is thoroughly cooked and tender.

Serve over white rice, topped with shredded Colby jack cheese.

24

BROILED STEAK SALAD

Broiled steak offers a chance for a great deal of the fat from the meat to leak into the broiler tray below, while not using the grilling that has been shown to cause some health considerations. Broiling meat and adding it to the wide array of greens and fresh vegetables ends up with a healthy and delicious meal that is gluten free and oh-so delicious.

You will need:
   4 tablespoons of olive oil

. . .

Main Dish Gluten Free Recipes.

6 teaspoons of apple cider vinegar 1 teaspoon fresh cilantro, chopped

2tablespoons of fresh parsley, finely chopped 1 bell pepper sliced in strips

3finely chopped green onions 1 clove garlic, minced

2 Roma or other meaty tomato, diced salt and pepper to taste.

2 cups romaine lettuce 2 cups iceberg lettuce 2 cups baby spinach

1/2 cup raw mushrooms

1/4 cup part skim mozzarella cheese 2 sirloin or Delmonico steaks

To make:

Take one quarter of the garlic, and rub steaks.

Salt and pepper steaks to taste, and place below the broiler. Allow steaks to broil turning once until cooked to your taste. Tear greens, mix and set aside.

Combine remaining ingredients and set aside.

Remove steaks from the broiler and cut into strips about half an inch wide Place greens into salad plates and top with strips of the steak.

Sprinkle with grated mozzarella

Drizzle the vegetable dressing over the steak and the salad greens till coated. Serve warm.

25

HEARTY STEAK AND CHEESE SOUP

Steak soup is a hearty way to end the day and perfect for those cooler autumn or winter days. If you're ready for a warm ending to the day, you can add the veggies and meats to your crock pot and leave on low heat for about 6 hours and your soup will be ready for you when you arrive home after work.

. . .

Main Dish Gluten Free Recipes.

Fresh raw vegetables are the best that you can get and will give your soup a wonderful flavor, but in the event that your raw veggies are off season, frozen vegetables will work nearly as well and most of the time does not cause the nutrients to erode. If you're really hungry, consider adding some canned or dried beans to your soup To make it a bit more hearty and rib-sticking.

You will need:

2 lbs. stew meat or diced steak 2 quart cans of tomato juice
    2 cups beef broth 1/4 cup frozen corn
    1/3 cup chopped green onion 1/3 cup chopped celery hearts
1 cup halved baby carrots
    1 cup diced potatoes 1 cup tomatoes diced
    1 cup whole green beans-raw 2 tsp. Sea salt
    freshly ground black pepper
    1 clove garlic-finely chopped 1/2 cup chopped green pepper
    1 cup shredded cheddar or Colby Jack cheese to top the soup.

To make:

Into 1 qt. of water put beef and boil for 1 hour on medium heat.
    For a hearty, substantial soup, cut up the meat in small pieces and add salt and pepper to taste.

Add tomatoes, tomato juice, onions and celery. Also add other vegetables, such as diced potatoes, carrots, string beans, corn, peas, cabbage or chopped peppers.

. . .

PAMELA KENDRICK

Boil until all vegetables are tender.

Serve topped with shredded cheddar and then broil it for just a moment To make the cheese bubbly.

26

BEEF AND BROCCOLI

One of the favorite Chinese foods which can be created is the beef and broccoli that we all eat on our forays out to the Chinese restaurant. This recipe can be made gluten free and also a bit healthier by the removal of a few things and the addition of another set. Keeping your foods heart healthy as well as gluten free means not using some of the traditional Chinese food inclusions such as monosodium glutamate, but in many cases, with the right spices, you're not even going to miss it.

It typically comes as a surprise to people that soy sauce is not gluten free traditionally. Soy sauce does tend to have wheat in it, but you can get around that with several brands of soy sauce that are fermented naturally and do not include gluten. The gluten free soy sauce has the same great taste that you'd come to expect. While we did name a brand that we know to be gluten free, bear in mind that there are others and this is simply a guideline.

You will need:

1 pound lean beef, sliced thinly into bite-sized pieces.

Marinade for Beef:
1 egg

1/3 tsp salt

1 Tbsp stock

1 Tbsp cornstarch (corn flour) 2 Tbsp water

Remaining Ingredients:

1 1/2 Tbsp sunflower oil

Main Dish Gluten Free Recipes.

116 ounce bag of broccoli, 1 cup sunflower oil

2Tbsp Kikkoman Gluten-Free Soy Sauce 1 Tbsp sugar

a few drops of sesame oil 2 cloves garlic, crushed 1/2 cup chicken broth

2 Tbsp cornstarch

To make:

Slice your beef into tiny pieces and add it to the marinade. Marinate the beef for at least half hour before adding the 1 1/2 tablespoons of oil to beef, mixing it all in and marinating your beef for another half hour.

While the beef is getting ready in the marinade, you'll be using that time to prepare the vegetables.

Heat a wok or a heavy pot and add 1 cup of oil. Stir fry the beef and remove it, setting it aside on another plate. Drain the oil and wipe it clean of oil. Add one half cup of water to your pot and bring it to a boil, adding the broccoli to it. Cover and cook the broccoli after coming to a boil for about 5 minutes. Drain and remove the broccoli.

Heat the pan or wok with about 2 tablespoons of oil. Add the garlic and fry lightly. Add the veggies, the beef and mix them thoroughly. In the center of the pan, make a well of sorts and add all of the ingredients for the sauce. Stir the cornstarch into a tablespoon of water and use this to thicken your broth. Mix the sauce together with the other ingredients and serve hot accompanied by rice if you like.

27

CURRIED CHICKEN AND MANGO SUMMER SALAD

Not only gorgeous because of the color, it's light and easy to accomplish for a summer meal. The main things which require any cooking are the chicken which can easily be broiled or grilled, keeping the kitchen heat to a minimum. Adding the mango to the meal makes it colorful and pretty, as well as lowering the calories and adding some phytonutrients. The yogurt adds a good dose of probiotics to your meal and all in all, this is one of the more healthy summertime quick meals you're going to find.

. . .

Main Dish Gluten Free Recipes.

You will need:

3/4 cup plain Greek yogurt Juice of one half lime
2 teaspoons clover honey 1 teaspoon curry
1/8 teaspoon sea salt

1/8 teaspoon freshly ground pepper

2 cups cooked broiled chicken, cut into bite sized pieces 1 cup mango peeled and cubed
About 10 leaves of Romaine lettuce

To make the salad:

Combine the first six ingredients in the list into a small bowl and stir it all really well.
Add the chicken and mango pieces and toss to coat.
On a salad plate, layer several leaves of crunchy Romaine.
Spoon the mango chicken mixture onto the top of the lettuce leaves and add a
few pieces of chopped celery or cucumber for pretty and for crunch.

This delicious summer salad is also low in fat, low in calories and incorporates all of the health benefits that yogurt and mango have to offer.
Health Challenges in Our World

In the world today, some of the biggest challenges to our health include heart disease, stroke, Alzheimer's, cancer, and type 2 diabetes. Many of these things can be warded off if our diet becomes healthier and a little more natural. That means removing high fat foods, some of which are also high in gluten and replacing those foods with more natural foods such as fruits, vegetables and flour which is made of healthier ingredients. Whole grain foods are healthy in and of themselves, but once processed, contain additives which can be cancer- causing and high in fat.

Eliminating some of those foods can help To make a very positive change in your lifestyle and in your health. It may promote long term weight loss and change your life for the better. Adding more raw vegetables and even cooked or steamed will add further benefits to your long term good health.

SIDE DISHES AND VEGETABLES

Vegetables are a very healthy part of your diet. So far as possible eating your vegetables raw is usually preferable in order to keep the nutrients sound. Many of the vitamins and minerals do not stay well during cooking or storage, with some being very unstable.

While there are exceptions to this rule, which will be named later, for the most part, keeping your vegetables raw will keep them more nutritious. Side dishes and salads are a very healthy part of your diet, combating some kinds of cancer as well as adding phytonutrients to your diet.

28

WINTER SQUASH IN BROWN BUTTER AND PARSLEY

Since this side-dish is prepared on the stovetop, it is especially nice for Thanksgiving and Christmas, when oven space always seems to be limited.

You will need:

. . .

1 ½ pounds winter squash, peeled, seeded, and cut into ½ inch cubes. (Acorn, or Butternut squash work well.)

4 Tbsp real butter

1 ½ Tbsp chopped, fresh parsley

¼ tsp salt

¼ tsp freshly ground black pepper 1 Tbsp brown sugar (optional)

To make:

Place butter in a large skillet over medium heat, stirring frequently with a whisk. Once melted, the butter will foam a little, subside, milk solids will form and become a honey brown color. At this time the butter will have a strong nutty smell. (It take just a few seconds for your browned butter to burn, if this happens, you'll need to start over.) Once the butter is browned, remove pan from heat and stir in fresh parsley.

Add cubed squash to pan, and turn to coat pieces evenly with butter, return to medium heat.

Allow the squash to cook on on side until it is lightly browned. This usually takes a few minutes. Continue turning squash to evenly brown all sides.

Reduce heat to low, and cover. Let squash cook until fork tender, around ten minutes.

Add brown sugar, if desired, just before squash is done, and turn to distribute

evenly.

29

CHINESE GREEN BEANS

We all love those delicious green beans that we get in the Chinese restaurant. The secret is the sesame oil in many cases, and you can make the same thing at home in a really short time. Using gluten free soy sauce, sesame oil and a few other ingredients, you can get all the taste that you want and absolutely none of the gluten that might be found in a restaurant offering. Try out this recipe for Chinese green beans and you may never have to find them at the restaurant again.

You will need:

. . .

1 pkg frozen green beans , one pound 1 tablespoon gluten free soy sauce

 1 can gluten free chicken broth 1 bunch green onions, about six 2 cloves of garlic

 1/4 tsp ground ginger 1 tsp sugar

 1 tbsp sesame oil

To make:

In a 2-quart casserole dish, combine green beans and broth. Cover and microwave 4 minutes on high. Make sure that your dish is microwave safe and remove it with an oven mitt.

Meanwhile, chop the onion and mince garlic.

 Into a small bowl, put the ginger, soy sauce and sugar.

 Add scallion rings and garlic. Set aside. Remove green beans from microwave and uncover.

 Pour sauce over beans and stir.

 Add to the microwave again for approximately 3 minutes. Remove and ensure they are heated through. Stir in the sesame oil and serve immediately.

30

HIGH ENERGY BREAKFAST SMOOTHIE

Smoothies or breakfast shakes can be a very healthy way to start your day when you're in a hurry, as we all are in the morning. Getting a good dose of veggies and fruits in a way that everyone can enjoy means that you start your day with a good breakfast, avoid all the gluten, not to mention the sugar, that you're going to get from a normal wheat-laden breakfast and you'll have the energy you need to face the morning.

You will need:

. . .

PAMELA KENDRICK

One medium sized banana 1 slice fresh pineapple
 1/4 cup fresh blueberries 1/4 cup sliced strawberries 1 cup skim milk
 1 tablespoon honey

To make:

Simply combine all ingredients and blend till smooth in a high speed blender.

31

HEART HEALTHY SPINACH SIDE SALAD

Salad is a very healthy side dish and is almost always gluten free, depending on the dressing that you get. This side salad features some very heart healthy additions and also greens which have been chosen for their nutritional phytonutrients. Additionally the presence of lycopene in the tomatoes as well as the Omega fatty acids which are found in the sunflower seeds offers you a real boost to your health.

PAMELA KENDRICK

. . .

You will need:
    2Roma tomatoes-quartered in wedges 2 cups Romaine lettuce
    2 cups baby spinach leaves 2 cups iceberg lettuce
    2 chopped green onions

1 cucumber, sliced in thin slices 2 tablespoons sunflower seeds

For the dressing:

One quarter cup olive oil

One quarter cup red wine vinegar 1 clove garlic, finely chopped
    1 teaspoon cilantro chopped

1 teaspoon parsley , finely chopped

To make:

Combine the dressing ingredients and set aside. Allow to come to room temperature.

Quarter tomatoes.

Slice cucumbers carefully.

. . .

Side Dishes and Vegetables

Break up the greens and alternate layers in two salad bowls.

Lay several tomato and cucumber slices arranged on top of the greens.

Shake the dressing gently to mix all ingredients and drizzle over the top of the greens and tomatoes.

Sprinkle liberally with sunflower seed.

Note. Tomatoes are very healthy; chock full of a nutrient called lycopene. The lycopene is a very good "anti-cancer" booster, but it requires either being cooked or a small amount of oil to be absorbed well. The olive oil in this salad dressing is actually a booster that will help the tomatoes to offer even more health benefits.

32

CREAMY BROCCOLI AND CAULIFLOWER SALAD

The tastes of raw broccoli and cauliflower were just made for summer time. This is an amazing taste treat and is also remarkably healthy. Cruciferous vegetables such as broccoli and cauliflower are not only heart healthy but may actually combat cancer and are high in vitamin A.

. . .

Side Dishes and Vegetables

As quickly as this salad can be created and tasty as it is you may well find the perfect way to assure that your children will eat their veggies even in the summer time. The creamy taste of the salad comes from the slight amount of sour cream, but if you're concerned with calories, you'll get the same taste from a low fat sour cream. In order to create this salad, a small amount of milk can be used to thin the dressing slightly if needed.

You will need:

One head of broccoli-chopped (not the stems) One head of cauliflower, cored and chopped

1/2 pound of precooked bacon,(about six slices) fried and chopped or crumbled

1/8 cup green onion very finely chopped

1/2 cup frozen green peas, thawed, but not cooked 1/2 cup grated cheddar cheese

1 cup mayonnaise or salad dressing 1/2 cup sour cream

To make:
Combine sour cream and Salad Dressing and thin slightly with milk till consistency of a thick salad dressing.

Combine all remaining ingredients and toss together in bowl. Pour salad dressing over and toss lightly.

Allow to sit in refrigerator so that your flavors can begin to blend slightly before you serve the salad.

33

HEARTY SUMMER SALAD

Brunch or summertime meals can be difficult for those who are gluten intolerant or eat a gluten free diet. Cookouts often mean that you're getting foods such as hamburgers which incorporate gluten laden ingredients and may also require buns. Gluten free can be a bit more difficult when trying to whip up a cool and easy summertime meal which doesn't require a lot of cooking.

This chickpea and black eyed pea salad is amazingly healthy and refreshing for those days when you just can't even look at the stove. High in protein and in fiber, you'll be well nourished while getting a break from the day to day cooking grind on those hot summer days.

Side Dishes and Vegetables

. . .

You will need:

2 of the 15 oz. cans chickpeas

2 of the 15 oz. cans black-eyed peas 2-15 oz. cans artichoke hearts 4 large tomatoes

½ large onion

3 large fresh garlic cloves

¼ cup olive oil

½ cup balsamic vinegar

A few pinches parsley Fresh ground salt Pepper to taste 1/4 cup green olives 1/4 teaspoon dried basil

To make:

Drain the beans and add to a bowl.

Chop the artichoke hearts into 8 pieces each and add to the mixture. Chop tomatoes or dice them into pieces.

Dice your onion and add to the mixture. Crush the garlic and mince it very finely. Drain olives and add to the mixture.

Chop the parsley finely. Add the basil.

Mix your vinegar and olive oil To make a lovely topping. Drizzle the dressing over the top.

Allow to cool in the refrigerator to blend your flavors for about an hour.

APPETIZERS AND SNACKS

It's difficult at times to find gluten free snacks and treats that you can serve at the afternoon Super Bowl Party or just for a quick snack. Most of the processed foods have come into contact with gluten in some way. If you're concerned about making sure that you're not going to be touched by a gluten product or you'd simply like to know how To make your own gluten free treats for a party, we've got a special section of snacks and appetizers for you to create.

Chicken wings are one of our favorite treats. If you're like us, the taste is great and a few of those delectable little bites are just right for an afternoon snack or a small finger food to be served up while you watch the big game. Two different varieties of chicken wings, each of them gluten free are offered here.

Our Chicken Wing recipes have it all. Great taste, lower fat, and just the right amount of heat.

34

GARLIC AND PARMESAN CHICKEN WINGS

You will need:

One small can parmesan cheese (8 ounces) 1 teaspoon garlic powder
  2 teaspoons sea salt, ground finely 1 stick margarine
  1/2 teaspoon pepper

· · ·

2 tablespoons corn meal

4 pounds chicken wings, cut up into pieces, with tips discarded

To make:

Preheat oven to 400 degrees
   Place all ingredients except the margarine and chicken wings into a plastic zip lock bag
   Shake to blend ingredients.

Lightly roll chicken wing into margarine and dip into the seasoning. Place on foil lined cookie or baking sheet.
   Sprinkle remaining seasonings over the top of your chicken wings and drizzle with margarine.

Bake at 400 until browned and completely done, approximately 30 minutes in preheated oven.
   Test with meat thermometer to ensure proper temperature.

35

HOT AND SPICY CHICKEN WINGS

A little on the spicy side, you'll want to ensure that you have some milk or tomato juice on hand for those who may be affected by the heat in these.

You will need:

2 ounces of Louisiana hot sauce or hot pepper sauce 1/4 cup of ketchup
1/4 cup brown sugar 1 stick butter
1 teaspoon garlic powder sea salt grinder
freshly ground pepper

To make:

Layer chicken wings on foil covered baking sheet.
Brush lightly with butter and season to taste with salt and pepper.

Mix the remaining ingredients together and thoroughly brush over chicken wings.

Bake at 400 approximately 30-40 minutes until done through.

Tips on Snackable Treats:
Did you know that the FDA of the United States considers that fruits which have been frozen are comparable in nutrition to those which are fresh and they allow frozen fruit to be labeled as fresh fruit and considered to be healthy. Frozen fruit is already washed and is ready to eat.

Fruit is naturally gluten free and the cleaning the prepping has already been done for you. To enjoy a fast To make treat, take several of your favorites and add them to a smoothie. The phytonutrients as well as the fiber are incredibly good for you, in some cases even helping to detox the body and to give you some amazing nutrients and health benefits. Many fruits actually help to fight cancers of various types and can be used to protect your long term health.

Fruit is gluten free in most cases and it's just plain good for you. Snack on some fresh fruit or even frozen in order to stave off hunger and get a fast and easy gluten free snack.

36

GLUTEN FREE CONSERVES AND RELISHES

Sometimes it's difficult to buy things like cranberry sauce and various types of relish which are not gluten free or aren't guaranteed not to have come into contact with gluten on machinery. Making your own eliminates that risk and gives you a fresher and more delicious product. One of the hardest things to find is a relish that doesn't have additives or glutens such as you will find in many of the different processed relishes and conserves. It's easy to create your own from fresh fruits and vegetables as well as to add other ingredients which are healthy and natural. Why take a chance on the jarred or canned items when you can make your own very easily and in a relatively short amount of time.

37

RAW SALSA

Salsa is one of our favorite things. Having had some contact with other ethnic groups over time, we've found that most Hispanics do not use the kind of salsa that we do, but rather make it fresh and raw at nearly every meal. We became very accustomed to this kind of salsa and really prefer it to the jarred variety. This recipe for raw salsa is heart healthy, free of gluten and absolutely delicious.

38

HOME MADE SPICY SALSA

You will need:

6 Roma or other meaty tomatoes 6 green onions
2 cloves of garlic 1 jalapeno
1 can chopped green chilies Handful of chopped cilantro 1 chopped bell pepper
1 teaspoon fresh lime juice 1/4 teaspoon ground sea salt Dash of pepper

Appetizers and Snacks

To make:

Chop the tomatoes into small squares.

Finely chop remaining ingredients except for the jalapeno and add to the mixture.

Determine how hot you would like your salsa to be. Add one quarter, one half or one full jalapeno, depending upon your preference for heat.

Remove the seeds and chop the pepper finely, adding the portion that you would like.

Refrigerate your salsa for about 2 hours to allow the flavors to blend nicely.

39

CRANBERRY CONSERVE

Cranberry conserve is an old style way to use cranberries. It's a great changeover from the old jellied cranberry sauce that many people serve at the holiday. In our house, there is no such thing as a cranberry sauce that comes from a can. The risk that some of these items have come in contact with gluten is one that we would prefer not to take.

While this is wonderful at the holidays, it's also a super addition to nearly any meal and tastes great when used on burgers for a fresh

Appetizers and Snacks

new style. This is an old Amish recipe which has been rewritten To make it a bit easier To make and to store.

You will need:

4 cups of fresh cranberries 2 large oranges-sliced
 1cup chopped raisins (* you may prefer the golden variety of raisins)
 2cups of water

3cups pure cane sugar

1/2 cup chopped nuts (optional, and we normally omit

these. If you know of anyone with a nut allergy, avoid them).

To make:

Slice the oranges and discard the seeds
 Grind the fresh cranberries and oranges, in a blender or chopper Transfer it to a heavy sauce pan and add the water.
 Cook the fruit rather quickly on a higher fire, being careful to prevent scorching.

Add sugar and raisins. Cook the mix over medium to low heat, stirring the conserve very often, until it begins to thicken.

. . .

PAMELA KENDRICK

This freezes very well and can be kept in the refrigerator for up to 14 days.

GLUTEN FREE DESSERTS

Healthy gluten free desserts are recipes are much sought after. In many cases, getting chocolate means that it is accompanied by other things that those who need to stay strictly gluten free cannot eat. We can't stress enough that you are going to need to really review cans and ingredients to ensure that your cocoa and other items have not been made on shared equipment and in places where wheat or gluten is present in tiny amounts.

In many cases, although we're uncertain why it is so, the brand names will be made on shared equipment while those which are not major brands will be cleaner and less likely to have contaminants. Check every label carefully to ensure that your products are gluten free and have not had the chance of being contaminated by other products which may contain gluten.

40

HOT CHOCOLATE PUDDING

Not only delicious, but also quite healthy with its touch of cocoa powder, containing phytonutrients that are actually proven to combat some types of cancer, your dessert will be luscious and nutritional, while at the same time being gluten free.

Hot Chocolate pudding is one of the most delicious desserts that you're going to find. It's easy To make and takes about 15 minutes from start to finish.

. . .

PAMELA KENDRICK

You will need:

2/3 cup pure cane sugar

2 tablespoons of corn starch pinch of salt
    1 and 1/2 cups canned milk 1 and 1/2 cups water
    4 egg yolks, slightly beaten 1/2 tsp. real vanilla
    6 ounce bar of Hershey's Dark chocolate 1 tsp. Hershey's cocoa

To make:

Combine your sugar, the corn starch and the salt.
    Adding about a fourth of a cup of milk, make a very smooth paste-like substance.
    Add the remainder of the milk and your egg yolks, stirring til completely blended.

Put the pan over medium heat stirring constantly until it begins to thicken. Pour into dessert cups and allow to set up about ten minutes.
    Transfer into refrigerator or serve warm with a bit of cocoa sifted lightly over the top.

41

RICE PUDDING

Rice pudding, particularly warm rice pudding is a favorite of nearly everyone who tastes it. Topped with cinnamon it becomes a very healthy ending to your gluten free meal.

You will need:

4 egg yolks

2/3 cup granulated sugar 3 cups of milk
    2 tablespoons of corn starch 1/2 tsp. pure vanilla extract 1/4 cup raisins (optional) 3/4 cups of instant rice
    dash of cinnamon

To make the rice pudding:

Make the instant rice in the microwave according to package directions. When making it during the last minute of cooking drop in the raisins into the rice to steam and soften them.

In a saucepan, combine the cornstarch, the sugar, and the egg yolks.

Stir until smooth, adding a slight amount of milk as necessary to thin the mixture down to a smooth paste.
    Add the remaining milk and stir to combine all ingredients.

Cook over low heat for approximately 12 minutes until the mixture thickens. Do not boil.

Remove from heat and allow cooling approximately 5 minutes. Drain any remaining water from the rice and raisins.
    Combine the rice with the pudding mixture and spoon into dessert dishes. Dust the top with cinnamon if desired.

42

CHOCOLATE FONDUE

Dark chocolate has made some big news recently for the fact that it is one of the newest--and the most taste tempting heart healthy foods. Dark chocolate keeps more of the flavonoids than the other varieties. New research is telling us that dark chocolate with its flavonoid content can help to keep your heart healthy and to prevent some types of cardiovascular diseases. Fortunately dark chocolate, which is rich in flavonoids is not rich in gluten--and remains one of the most delicious foods that you can eat which is gluten free.

Obviously that doesn't mean that you can ignore the high calorie content and dash to the store to get yourself a ton of dark chocolate to the exclusion of other kinds of food, but it does mean that when eaten in moderation as part of a healthy diet, dark chocolate can help you to stay healthier in the long term.

Dark Chocolate Fondue

You will need:

12 ounces Dark Chocolate finely chopped 3/4 cup heavy Whipping Cream
Fresh strawberries Fresh pineapple Fresh blueberries Sliced bananas Fresh sliced apples

To make:

Heat the whipping cream until very warm and drop the chocolate into the whipping cream.
Allow all chocolate to melt thoroughly and stir til smooth, but do not allow boiling.
Keep warm over a pot of warm water in a double boiler and using toothpicks or bamboo skewers and dip the fresh fruit into the chocolate pot.

43

CHOCOLATE CAKE

Also called by some, gluten free soufflé, this is one of the most decadent desserts that you will create which is gluten free. One taste and you're absolutely in love. Much more like a chocolate soufflé than it is a cake; the taste is out of this world. The cocoa adds some antioxidants to your dessert, keeping you healthier and helping to stave off some long term disease processes.

. . .

You will need:

2 sticks of butter (you must use real butter for this recipe, not margarine which is slightly more watery)

1/4 cup Hershey's unsweetened cocoa, plus one teaspoon for dusting the pan

8 ounces of bitter, mildly sweetened chocolate, chopped into fine pieces 5 eggs

1 and 1/4 cups heavy whipping cream 1 cup pure cane sugar

1/2 cup sour cream

1/4 cup powdered sugar

To create the cake:

Preheat your oven to 350 degrees Fahrenheit Butter a spring form pan measuring 9 inches.

Melt the butter and combine with the quarter cup of heavy cream until it is all melted.

Add the chocolate bars and allow melting. Stir to smooth the mixture and remove it from the heat.

Beat eggs, sugar and cocoa into the chocolate into the buttered pan, add the batter you've just created and bake until the entire mixture is set and puffed up. It will take about 40 minutes to cook completely.

Allow to cool approximately 40 minutes to an hour before you try to unmold the cake.

Beat the sour cream and the confectioners' sugar with the remaining heavy cream and serve as a sauce.

Decadent does not even begin to describe this dessert, which is lovely enough to serve to guests at a holiday dinner.

44

BAKED APPLES

With walnuts which are heart healthy, as well as the cinnamon, these can be a healthy part of your diet. Walnuts which contain the omega fatty acids are a good part of a healthy diet. Desserts don't have to be unhealthy. While the butter adds a small amount of saturated fat to your diet, it is so slight as to be negligible.

. . .

Gluten Free Desserts

You will need:

4 apples, preferably Cortland or Spies 1/4 cup brown sugar
    5 teaspoons water

1/4 teaspoon cinnamon

2 tbsp. real butter, cut into slices Walnuts or pecans for garnish, as desired

To make baked apples:

Preheat the oven to 375 degrees.

Core the apples, removing the seeds and slice the bottom off so that they lay flat in the baking dish.

Place each apple in the pan.

Drop a small pat of butter inside each apple.

Mix the brown sugar and the water To make a slightly thick syrup.

Drip the syrup over the apples and bake them for approximately 20-30 minutes.

PAMELA KENDRICK

Take the sauce from the dish and spoon over the warm apple. Serve with ice cream or whipped cream if desired.

45

COFFEE CHOCOLATE MOUSSE

Chocolate mousse is another of those decadent dessert treats that will leave you feeling very satisfied. You're not going to know that you're missing gluten at all with desserts like these, which make wonderful desserts for dinner parties or for the perfect holiday meal.

You will need:

. . .

One Hershey's Special (tm) dark bar 8 ounce size 3 egg yolks, slightly beaten
    2 teaspoons instant coffee 6 tablespoons sugar
    2 cups whipping cream

To create the mousse:

Melt your chocolate into a bowl over water or in a double boiler. Stir once in a while until smooth.

In a small pan, whip your egg yolks, coffee powder and 3/4 cup of the whipping cream, as well as 4 tbsp. of granulated sugar.

Heat thoroughly, stirring all the while for about three minutes, but do not allow the mixture to completely boil.

Add the mixture to the chocolate mixture, stirring until smooth and glossy. Cool completely, refrigerating if necessary for about half an hour.
    Using your mixer beat the cream and the remaining sugar until it is forming stiff peaks.
    Fold in one third of the chocolate mix, then the second, and finally the third portion of it.

Pour into glass serving bowls and refrigerate until hard.

If desired, garnish with shaved chocolate or sifted cocoa powder.

GLUTEN FREE TIPS FOR FUN KID FOODS

It's difficult to have a child who requires a gluten free diet. In many cases, like their friends, they want to eat "normal" foods which can cause them some long term health problems. If you're one of the millions of moms who have a child requiring a gluten free diet, you can't change what they need, but you can change it To make their diet a bit more fun and interesting.

These ideas are based on some fun facts and some fun ideas for moms which can make meal time just a bit less of a struggle.

Gluten Free Breakfast Idea

Remember the old Dr. Seuss Books. One that was always a favorite was "Green Eggs and Ham." Make a child's sleepover a lot more fun and cover the fact that your child isn't eating the typical cereal by making a healthy and a fun breakfast of Green Eggs and Ham.

Just a few drops of food coloring will create a very festive meal of green eggs and ham, keeping your child--and his or her prospective company--away from the fact that there are not the typical sugary cereals at the breakfast table. Additionally you're adding some real nutritional value and keeping them clear of high sugar breakfast foods.

To turn scrambled eggs green, you'll want to use blue food coloring, while the green works well on the ham (turkey ham is better). Just a drop will do the job.

Gluten Free Chocolate Chip Cookies

Kids love chocolate chip cookies, but finding one that is gluten free and allows your child to enjoy the treats that other kids take for granted isn't always an easy task. Even some chocolate chips are processed on equipment that is not always free of the allergen that troubles them.

One answer to this is using buckwheat flour to create recipes. Despite its name, buckwheat is not true wheat. It is gluten free, according to the Celiac disease website and offers a lot of protein and iron on top of being gluten free.

Creating chocolate chip cookies from buckwheat, which is a good substitute for traditional flour makes them a tiny bit heavier but allows your kids to have the treat that they want, and you want to give them.

You will need:

1 and 1/4 cup buckwheat flour 1/2 tsp. soda
    1/2 tsp. salt

1 stick of butter

1/4 cup dark brown sugar 1/2 tsp. vanilla extract
    1 egg

1 cup chocolate chips (remember to check the package to ensure they are gluten free)

To make:

Combine the dry ingredients except the sugar Whip together softened butter, egg and sugar
    Mix the sugar mixture with the remaining dry ingredients and mix thoroughly.

Stir in chocolate chips
    Drop by rounded teaspoons onto a lined cookie sheet. Bake at 375 degrees for 9-12 minutes.

CROCK POT COOKERY AND GLUTEN FREE?

One of the questions that is most frequently asked is can I make gluten free recipes in the crock pot. The answer to that is a resounding yes. Most soups and stews are naturally gluten free, using only meats and vegetables. Your favorite recipes of any kind can be made in the crock pot to give you some easy ways to create a meal ahead of time.

Adapting recipes for your slow cooker.

Whether you are cooking traditional foods or gluten free foods, there are times when you want to prepare your food ahead of time and have it ready to go when you arrive at home. In most cases, vegetable and meat stews are going to be easier to prepare and can be made ahead of time to be ready for a hot meal if you're using a crock pot. Soups and stews can have all of the preparation work accomplished the night before and be placed in the crock pot to cook away while you do other things.

Most recipes can be adapted for the crock pot, offering a great way to leave your hands free in meal preparation. The advantages of the crock pot are that they offer you better meals, which are going to be healthier in nature and lower in fats than most of the fast food choices you might make.

Crock Pot Cookery and Gluten Free?

Here are a few tips for changing your recipes to crock pot ready recipes.

Bear in mind that if you're going to be using frozen veggies, they only need about half hour, so add them to your recipes for the last 40 minutes of cooking.

Soak dried items such as beans or lentils for an hour or so prior to adding them to the crock pot.

If the recipes require pasta, even gluten free pasta, that too should only be added in the last hour of cooking time.

Bear in mind that you want to lower the liquid amounts in crock pot cooking. You will want to lower them by about one quarter of the overall liquid recipe
since the lid doesn't allow for a vast amount of evaporation.

When using the crock pot, layering the veggies on the bottom and adding the meat to the top is the best plan of action.

If your recipe takes about 30 minutes cook time, it will take about 3 hours on high, 4 hours on medium, and 6 hours on low in the crock pot.

Restaurant Foods on a Gluten Free Diet

Eating out always has the potential to be difficult, but it can be particularly so when you are on any type of a restricted diet. Typically any meal that offers gravy is going to use a roux to thicken it, so make sure that you ask before you order that Sunday roast at a restaurant.

Many places today cater to gluten free people and do have a special menu that they can offer which allows for gravy and sauces which are made from corn flour rather than roux as a thickening agent.

Prior to heading out to a new restaurant a phone call may be in order to find out what kind of foods are available on the menu rather than hoping you find something you may be able to eat and finding out that you're wrong.

Nearly every restaurant serves fresh fruit of some type, but you'll want to be sure there is something else there that you can make a meal of rather than leaving it to chance.

If you find yourself in a restaurant on the spur of the

moment, there are some foods that usually do not require the addition of anything which may be gluten laden.

Some choices that you can make which are typically gluten free in the restaurants (although do ask to be sure) include:

Roast turkey Broiled Chicken Pork Chops Broiled Steaks

Fresh steamed veggies

Desserts are going to be the most difficult to get when you are on a gluten free diet, but bear in mind that your selections can include fruit salads, as well as

crème brulee, along with nearly any type of pudding which is typically made with corn flour as opposed to a flour thickening agent.

Make sure that you ask your server and if you do not get a satisfactory answer, do ask to speak with the chef in order to find out what kind of gluten free menu items the restaurant offers.

TIPS ON LIVING GLUTEN FREE

1.Many foods are naturally gluten free. You do not have to shop the fringe to find all gluten free foods. Things like rice noodles, buckwheat, fruits and veggies are gluten free naturally. Use those products and save some money on the cost of buying gluten free.

2.Use common sense. Many companies make a big production and a big payday by touting their foods as gluten free. There is even a gluten free rice. The rice grain is naturally gluten free so make sure you are aware of what foods are gluten free before paying more for a product that may be naturally gluten free.

3.Many stores carry a list of foods that are gluten free. Bigger shopping sites such as Trader Joe's, Wegmans and many other supermarkets will be glad to give you a list of gluten free goods and enable you To make great choices without searching the entire store.

4.Make sure you look for "gluten free" on the label. Gluten free and wheat free are two entirely different things and not all products which are free of wheat are also free of gluten.

5.Buy a few good books. Richard Coppedge, Jr, who is a professor of baking and pastry arts at The Culinary Institute of

Tips on Living Gluten Free

America is also the author of a book on gluten free baking that may become your new Bible. " Gluten-Free Baking With The Culinary Institute of America: 150 Flavorful Recipes From the World's Premier Culinary College.

6. Some types of oil may have been made on equipment which was shared with gluten containing products. Check the labels of everything, even those foods which you believe should be gluten free. It doesn't hurt to be a little extra careful.

7. Many companies today make foods which are already done and are gluten free. Check them for use in those moments when you need something fast and easy. Gluten free premade meals are available in most regular supermarkets today.

8. Online websites are one of the best places to find gluten free tips and new gluten free recipes. In fact, at last count there were about 5000 gluten free recipe sites which can be used to help you to supplement your meals and to get great substitutions for foods or products that contain gluten.

9. If you live in a small area, supermarkets and even companies such as Amazon are offering online gluten free products that you can order. Typically the shipping prices are quite low and you'll have the products within just a few days. If you live in an area where the supermarket is not large and gluten free products aren't part of what they carry, shopping online can be a life-saver.

10. Rice flour is amazing for fried foods. While it is gritty and often causes problems in bread, the rice flour for use when frying items or making tempura is a wonderful addition because that bit of extra texture is very welcome. Don't rule out rice flour all together when you're cooking because of the grit.

REFERENCES

We've made several statements during the course of the book which promote the use of broccoli, cauliflower, and other cruciferous vegetables being used in gluten free cooking to aid in detoxifying the body and to assist in adding fiber to the diet. These statements are made using references from the Pub Med materials and the Nutritional Journal references which can be found below.

Ambrosone CB, Tang L. Cruciferous vegetable intake and cancer prevention: role of nutrigenetics. Cancer Prev Res (Phila Pa). 2009 Apr;2(4):298-300.

Angeloni C, Leoncini E, Malaguti M, et al. Modulation of phase II enzymes by sulforaphane: implications for its cardioprotective potential. J Agric Food Chem. 2009 Jun 24;57(12):5615-22.

Banerjee S, Wang Z, Kong D, et al. 3,3'-Diindolylmethane enhances chemosensitivity of multiple chemotherapeutic agents in pancreatic cancer. 3,3'- Diindolylmethane enhances

References

chemosensitivity of multiple chemotherapeutic agents in pancreatic cancer.

Bhattacharya A, Tang L, Li Y, et al. Inhibition of bladder cancer development by allyl isothiocyanate. Carcinogenesis. 2010 Feb;31(2):281-6.

Bryant CS, Kumar S, Chamala S, et al. Sulforaphane induces cell cycle arrest by protecting RB-E2F-1 complex in epithelial ovarian cancer cells. Molecular Cancer 2010, 9:47.

Christopher B, Sanjeez K, Sreedhar C, et al. Sulforaphane induces cell cycle arrest by protecting RB-E2F-1 complex in epithelial ovarian cancer cells. Molecular Cancer Year: 2010 Vol: 9 Issue: 1 Pages/record No.: 47.

Clarke JD, Dashwood RH, Ho E. Multi-targeted prevention of cancer by sulforaphane. Cancer Lett. 2008 Oct 8;269(2):291-304.

Cornelis MC, El-Sohemy A, Campos H. GSTT1 genotype modifies the association between cruciferous vegetable intake and the risk of myocardial infarction. Am J Clin Nutr. 2007 Sep;86(3):752-8.

Hu J, Straub J, Xiao D, et al. Phenethyl isothiocyanate, a cancer chemopreventive constituent of cruciferous vegetables, inhibits cap-dependent translation by regulating the level and phosphorylation of 4E-BP1. Cancer Res. 2007 Apr 15;67(8):3569-73.

Jiang H, Shang X, Wu H, et al. Combination treatment with resveratrol and sulforaphane induces apoptosis in human U251 glioma cells. Neurochem Res. 2010 Jan;35(1):152-61.

Special Thanks to WHFoods for their valuable information on

broccoli, cauliflower and other cruciferous vegetables as well as the reference materials to point us in the right direction.

The American Journal of Clinical Nutrition was an invaluable resource in the creation of this book. Find them online at http://ajcn.nutrition.org/

www.ingramcontent.com/pod-product-compliance
Lightning Source LLC
Chambersburg PA
CBHW071624080526
44588CB00010B/1262